THE SURVIVORS

By the same author
THE MASK OF PITY
THE STONES REMEMBER
WELSH VOICES (*editor*)
SCARS

The
Survivors

BRYN GRIFFITHS

LONDON

J. M. DENT & SONS LTD

First published 1971

© Bryn Griffiths, 1971

Made in Great Britain
at the
Aldine Press · Letchworth · Herts
for
J. M. DENT & SONS LTD
Aldine House · Bedford Street · London

821
G R 1

ISBN: 0 460 03998 9

FOR JOHN AND LYN HUGHES

CONTENTS

ACKNOWLEDGMENTS

Acknowledgments are due to the following publications, in which many of these poems have appeared:

Transatlantic Review
London Welshman
Tribune
Melbourne Herald
Poetry Review
The Independent
Westerly
The Critic
Meanjin Review

My acknowledgments and thanks are due also to the British Broadcasting Corporation, the Australian Broadcasting Commission and the Arts Council of Great Britain.

GOING AWAY

We were going away, Waterloo station fading
into the wintry darkness of dusk,
where the rails spear, converge and meet;
where the signals fall back on absence,
filling the space where once we were—
platforms, cold waiting rooms, the living street.

Pausing, a sudden panic of blood and bone
crossing the clamorous points, we stall,
caught by the staccato stammer of the tracks—
a snarl of metal between earth and sky—
as far voices cry, something strange, blurred,
not clearly heard in the nimbus of night's mystery.

We drive on south, into other futures, through
darkness dividing suburbs, cities, strangers,
as power houses pass in silent force
and small stations of the night slam by
the shuttering windows, shuddering the mind
with hope and doubt as the tracks clatter goodbye.

A frame of living I thought fixed forever
is breaking apart, fragmenting familiar time,
disappearing from our day.
And so all things end, the good years give way
to something new, different, maybe happiness
elsewhere in another time, another clime.

We were going away, into the dark, so goodbye
London, alleyways coiling away into memory;
December's sombre cloak of winter falls
about you, and weather wars against the windows—
a cold shrapnel of sleet starring the glass—
as far below the viaducts life goes on,

the sky falls in silence, streets glisten black
as cars hiss through rain, and lost hours live again.

[1]

It seems as if all my memoried departures
are merged into one this dying day:
I stare into nothing, drift back into the past,
and another, younger, 'I' lives in the glass.

But he is forever the stranger now,
too far away from this shadowed reality;
too distant a watching presence this night
from all the misty years of youth;
and yet he stirs something deep, something lost,
in the brief pang of awakened memory;

the first mystery of moving on, of worlds to be.
All my life I was leaving, going away,
leaving safe harbours for wilder seas;
and again it's goodbye far friends, forgotten love;
goodbye Wales, old cloth-capped man,
singing still, forever part of me!

STARS

That first night under new skies,
your skies, unknown constellations,
we collided like two stars,
spinning in the cool universe
of a curtained room of night,
merging into one fury of love,
our flesh flaming white on white.

Northward, eternities away,
a world went by out of mind.
Southward, under the slow wheel
of the Southern Cross where strange stars
march across the sky, we met in fire,
two alien elements, far stars,
flashing life through a transient sky.

LOOKING BACK

Through the window, the wire-screened eye
of this hot skull of a house, Australia
shimmers in a blast of sun,
blue sky, flies and dust,
and the red tiles of endless suburbia.
Can one make a pattern of this,
weave words from such thin threads,
make sense of the mind's desert?
I have tried, and failed, for I am not of this.
I need another landscape, a sense of history,
a place where rain falls on sombre valleys,
the salmon run in their good season,
the hills billow green to the sea.
I take you with me, Wales, wherever I go.

FROGS

The hour was late, and I was trying to sleep
in the bellowing Australian hills . . .
but there were frogs about . . . everywhere—

FROGS

The night seemed full of frogs, Australian frogs,
noisy frogs, like ducks with laryngitis,
booming away in one incredible chorus of croaks
through the damp darkness of the night.

Big frogs
small frogs   thin frogs
and
great   big   fat   frogs—

all yelling and having their say until
the night creaked like a rusty hinge.

The Philippine frogs climb trees, they say,
and Spanish frogs dance flamencos all day;
and some cynics sneer that English frogs
wear bowler hats, suspenders and spats;

and that American frogs smoke fat cigars,
drive big flashy cars, are all film stars,
and live in apartments—not mud-flats!

But not these frogs, the bawling bull frogs,
the frightening frogs of the Darling Range.
They were just simple, blunt, classless,
open-air, down-to-earth, sun-tanned—

FROGS

They were practical frogs, garrulous frogs,
footballing frogs and cricketing frogs,
no doubt discussing boxing, beer,
stocks and shares, and the Melbourne Cup.

	Just simple	
sailing	swimming	surfing
	and	
boozing	chundering	bulldusting
	frogs!	

Or maybe this was some kind of frog convention,
held, shall we say, to debate the situation
of migrant frogs, the virtues of green and pink
and purple frogs, and other matters of the day.

I could make no sense of that noisy company,
so I kept to my bed, the sheets over my head,
for I knew vast armies of frogs
lay out there in clamorous ambush. . . .

For these were Antipodean frogs, Philistine frogs,
frogs of the Southern Cross, worker frogs
and boss frogs, frogs to frighten the cats
and dogs and all the bush beasties away!

Never, ever, were there such ferocious frogs.

ABOS

'They don't fit in here, mate,'
the bronzed Australian said,
'the abos just don't fit in.'

We were watching some aborigines,
stick-thin, at drunken play
on the sleazy side of a town

shimmering in the sun of Australia
as the far beaches rang with people,
pleasure, the good life being lived.

'They're like prehistoric men,'
he said, 'lost out of their time,
and they've got to make way.'

Make way for what? Each year
their land constricts, deserts begin,
progress fouls the landscape.

Forty thousand years of freedom
under the Southern Cross degenerate
now into suffering and squalor

beneath some broken shards of tin
too pitiful to be called a shack.
This, for them, is civilization.

We watched the aborigines shamble on
down the street, staggering through
the bulling crowds, making way.

ACCEPT AND ENDURE

The first men were changed here by the brooding land,
warped into a difference lost in time;
the flesh whittled away from the taut bone
till the body knew its way.
The sun bored holes into their brains
and filled their exploding skulls with fear.
The stars sang down their dream and legend.
They learned to survive in the burning earth.
They heard the silent country's utterance:
Thus you accept me, thus you are changed,
for I am ancient and the first and last:
in me is the infinite mystery.
They became part and one with the wilderness.
And now the newcomers, dreaming
they master and change these timeless deserts,
are themselves being changed, adapted
to another make of man. . . . And they, too,
must learn to accept, endure and survive,
for their time will be triggered by stars
and the fused force hovering above
which is the last and infinite question mark.

[6]

THE QUIET ROOMS

Those long London nights we spent, my love,
where we caught and held a sudden flame of love
cupped in the shielding curve of our bodies,
stir in this day's memory still. I cannot

ever now blank the mind's window on the past,
draw no dark blinds on your known beauty,
for you burn clear for me as summer sunlight
through the year's mist which hazes memory.

Through the days and dead months you live on—
the warm brown beauty of your loved eyes,
your soft mouth on mine, your hidden lair,
the bright stars in the black universe of hair.

I know the white flash of your body passing near;
each lithe movement of your ivory flesh
evoking old desire, our once familiar fire;
each facet of the past caught like a frozen tear.

Again I see the many rooms, the quiet rooms,
where we lay in love; where you were wild with me
in the long and wanton nights of jewelled hours;
where my imagination still spins a world of fire.

Whom do they shelter now, secret and near?
Who lives and loves where our shades
twine and coil in the silent shadows?
No answer rings the distance to tell me here.

Ten thousand miles now separate and divide
what was once close and secret in our hearts.
But time and time must pass, the seasons die,
and distance end some day. We never left the city,

made the green country, for always, it seems,
it came to other rooms, quiet rooms, where we
could come together in yet another night,
locking the world away, and be one without fear.

The love we knew is now lost, part of the past,
but what I felt for you then in those far rooms,
those distant, timeless rooms, flames for you still,
fierce as ever, my dear, my dear, my dear!

GHOST OF SILENCE

I am the shape that shudders in the wind.
I am the ghost that stalks the wastelands,
the desert and silence of Australia.
I cry forever, haunting the burnt land,
from prehistoric past to present.
The black men, walking wild, heard my cry
and made of me bright myth and legend.
The white men, coming late, have learnt to fear me.
For I am fear, death's spectre, strange shade of light—
high summer, at noon, the heat stressed to screaming—
stalking forest, desert, and clouded skull.
I am shadow, caught by the eye's brief flash,
flickering into dry air, dark rooms, doorways;
almost alive again in the dead towns' dust.
I am nothing, half seen, nearly there—
the mind's blind terror hovering on rout—
disturbing clarity, creating doubt.
I am the mist of dawn and sunset—
the creak of trees, cry of wind, crack of wood.
I am lament, the old song of silence,
for I am the land's ghost and the shape of fear.

SYDNEY LACE

Such a mesh of tangled iron shackles
the surprised eye at first
with yet another memory of a dead day—
a day forever frozen in metal,
linking Paddington,
this Sydney suburb chiming of London,
with a corsetted century of cant,
a fading bitter age, not yet buried.
And yet an old charm lives on
in the black lace of balconies
still masking the worn faces
of the streets; a whorl of patterns
the eye cannot follow;
reminiscent of the fleshed lace
I caress so soft and slowly
in the late day as now,
shadowed from the stunning sun,
iron lace locks me
into knowledge of beauty here,
where our slow lust is stirred
by the sun's last heat.
My blind fingers search for meaning—
each new sensation in the rippling flesh—
across the black braille of a body—
across the silk of a body—
as the dying light spiders flame alive
again in the mind's sensual mesh. . . .
And yet the change wrought by time
on man and landscape still insists
a presence here, where beauty still remains.
From my window, high above the harbour,
the balconies and tiered terraces
spangle an old grace across roofs
and shabby streets to where the city,

shrugging skywards through
the mazy scree of concrete, neon
drops down to Rushcutters,
where still waters glisten,
boats rock, lovers walk the dusk.
Thus change is apparent, always, different;
dividing, yet comparing, making one.
And now, from water, like dreaming,
the eye climbs from far hammering
echoes to where incredible skies
drift and cloud into infinity—
to where space sings clear of clamour—
and then descends to night
and recognition of black lace
on balcony and soft white body.

LEAVING SYDNEY STATION

Faces drift, move off, into gloom
like stirrings in another room
where people ghost beneath bright lights
that exist, now, for them alone
till death shears the red life from the bone
and all into darkness are gone.
Time stills in this winter station;
you come alive in the night's
soundless sarabande of scurried flesh
caught in the mind's slow motion;
and your face drifts with those others—
lost men and women, the dead lovers—
as the train moves endlessly away,
gathering to leap into night,
leaving you behind in the day
where you existed long ago.
Another chapter ends, another begins,

and yet your last words
still ebb and flow
like a timeless tide in me
as I watch through the window
the world slide by in the windy night—
the million small stars of manlight
scattered across the vast dark land—
and seeing only you out there
in the universe of shadowed glass
as through the country of night we pass.
'Never again,' you said, 'never again
will we know what we know now.
We break the moment's crystal,
learn its pain, the broken shards of love
in the many beds where we have lain.'
And so I leave once more, make my way
to countries where I cannot stay,
for words must be found again
in the wide continent of my craft.
But still an old love our hour tolls,
a chiming of forgotten bells,
that we will meet again one day
in London, Paris, Watson's Bay.
The days will blur by like pages
in Time's gigantic book of hours;
our lives but brief sequences
half seen in the whirling years of words;
chapter into chapter will blend
as all our players
leave their stages;
and who can tell, in this old dream,
when and where each story will end.
And thus we move through shadow
and sunlight, searching for answers,
the 'I' crying to be free for flight—
battering like a frightened bird

in the banging box of the brain—
and finding love and fear, day and night,
travelling with us like an old refrain.
We live our swift hours, caught in this cage,
as this brute beauty of earth spins,
as always, from calm to clamour,
black to whiteness, from age to age. . . .
We meet and mate, match breath with breath,
yet know our destiny is death.
And so I journey into another night
on these worn familiar tracks again,
leaving you on the shores of a silent bay
in the far memory of a green day.
But life is to be lived, the dice cast,
for our love is lost and cannot last.

THE SURVIVORS

They will live in the wastelands
where each beating tick of life
will be blood for the bone
breath for the heart's crying
in the chiming silences
after the clouds have killed and gone

They will live not as they live now
in the sweet dream of drifting green
but as survivors in the stillness
beyond stillness after the storms
have waned into the whispering distances
where nothing will be as before

They will know little of warring pain
and the drifting mists of death
above the slack of poisoned seas
for they live too far from pain
in that far sanctuary of the south
where the world goes by out of life

They will hear the song of war
laments of the lost and dead
on the waves of air still rolling
and in that hearing then of war
the truth tolling the end of their time
and the coming of change

And after the detonations have died
into the radiant distances
from whence they came like strange
beats in the planet's pulse of life
they will flee the cities
for the wilderness of land and sea

They will live in the echoing hills
with all the songs of the dead
and walk the shores of silent seas
changed by the elements and years
until another slow cycle begins
and the sagas go sailing out again

They will be changed as the blood
is changed in the sighing winds
till the good life becomes legend
to be told about the campfires
through a long millennium's climb
They are the survivors: mankind

CELEBRATION

Sweet female body, now lying still,
how you cried seconds ago
and brought me to fill your flesh—
        moving slow—
sleek in the surging body's lash—
till your wild cries I could kill
with one last detonation
driving from the root. . . . This celebration
of the flesh, this soundless cry,
now sings and flowers in the still
silence where you lie—
        soft, slender, aglow—
          where you shuddered
such brief eternities ago!

VICTORIANA

The long streets lance a living corpse:
Melbourne at midday, quivering in the sun,
still shackled by censors, custom,
pretension and tea cosies,
still beating the same old drum.

A paradox, a warped cross of commerce
with culture sprawled across

the dusty drain of a river,

the city mauls the landscape
with the drab monstrosities of another day.

Queen Victoria made a hit here,
and she lives on still,

                    spawning gloom,
a lingering parasite of the past,

threatening dire ends, damnation and doom,
from all the usual dreary sources.

She imprisoned so many in the legacy
of a dead imperium—
the withering cage of conformity—
and they bore us still in
the brainless battalions of Toorak's tedium.

So kill that queen, Melbourne, before
she murders the generations yet to come!

THE OUTBACK

      A continent of fire, salt and sand,
      debris of the drowned generations
      brazed and dormant to the sun's demand,
      the Outback sleeps on in silence,
      as in all the empty centuries,
      shimmering back at the iron sky
      a mute reply to the questioning stars.
      The elements of change, sun and stars,
      burn down the years more brilliant here;
      making a myth of mirage;
      setting starlight to the dreamtime;
      triggering death's cold word clear
      from the witching rainbow
      as the sun's rays splinter
      and ricochet into nothing.

But the land accepts the boned man,
the brute fury of blood-feud,
the weight of the terrible ages
pressing down, crying aloud
through the thunderous silence of noon.
Sometimes the colours of sun
and rain blaze again
from the land's mask of green,
after the siege of the year's storm,
and splash a sudden splendour across
the worn landscape, obeying then
the strictures of an old command. . . .
And yet nothing is soft, gives way,
makes easy for man his marching dream.
This harsh wanton of the earth,
this tawny torso spread gigantic
and forever against the sea's blue bed,
sucks dry the dawn webs of drifting air
and waits to draw back
into her ancient womb the brief seeds
of men who venture there.
The Outback is not for men,
the skies seem to cry,
for here all meaning fades
as the blasting sun
burns out their sweat
to wet barren earth, and scars their minds
with memories of the gold days
and ghost towns, where only a sigh
of wind now lingers there.

Here, in this painted desert of the brain,
men are changed and warped
to a different shape of being,
and women are withered before their time.
So we cling to the green frontier

of existence, blind to the beauty
of all the forgotten dreamtimes,
and the land endures while man passes on.

THE NULLABOR

The land is vertical.
A terrible wall of wasteland,
worn seabed of forgotten ages,
reaching endlessly towards
the vast blue roof of the sky
under which we travel, entrained,
through the dead belly of Australia.
To the side, through double windows,
far horizons march away
into the land's vacuum. . . . And yet,
for me, the train flees downhill
towards the sea.
                    Logic creeps in,
insists a cold presence,
states that this is desert—
                    horizontal—
the dry and dusty Nullabor
which we cross; that wall is floor;
that up is up and down is down,
and yet gravity nails us to a *wall*
nails the spinning feet
of this centipede of steel
to the miles of nothing.
We crawl on, articulated,
                    moving slow
across stone and sand,

caged in this trap of metal
till we hurtle down to drop and drown
in that distant sea.
                    Logic's ally,
my compartment's companion,
only sees the flat land, saltbush,
the lonely outposts of passing
humanity, and drinks his afternoon tea.
And yet for me,
lost in that huge immensity,
we fall downhill towards the sea.

TERRA INCOGNITA
Kalamunda, Australia, 1968

The sky is ablaze with cold light tonight:
a spangled multitude of stars look down
and make nothing of man, all space, all time.

What can one write of and make true here?
There is no history, no racial heritage,
nothing to make meaning of yet.

The night lies still and huge as eternity,
a cloak of shadow and silence shot with light,
across the dry acres of this vast harsh land.

This is *Terra Incognita*, the old mystery,
and I, like many before me, must search
that other unknown continent within.

From these hills, these worn fangs of stone
serrating the skyline of night,
the myriad lights of the distant city—

glittering white spark on white spark—
are small campfires where transient aliens
huddle afraid, as always, of the dark.

What can I sing of, make music of, here?
I ask the far stars in the blue-black sky,
but they burn back at me in brilliant

silence from that gigantic dark. . . .
The pioneers have long gone, into folklore,
all colour and spirit lost in their wake;

and now the people here build wall on wall,
raping the old landscape with an old greed,
as they drive back the slow tides of time;

while about them sweep the silent seas
of desert and bush, waiting for life, where
they cling to the safe edge of sanity.

They build in blindness a tinsel society,
thin as tissue, covering a vacuum of fear;
and man also has a desert in his heart.

These are the far wastelands of our world,
where we may yet find some future meaning
on the frontiers of the last wilderness,

but I can only map the present here,
and set down my small score of experience
to chart my days, for I, too, am transient.

WAR OF LOVE

My love now moves in marching war with me.
I wheel upon the bed's white plain as we
meet and I breach the blonde frontier of her flesh
which tangles all thought in a timeless mesh.

Her mouth guns the loaded charges in the brain
as my breath collides with her soft calls of pain.
She bends beneath the salient of my lust,
drives my heart's loud drumbeat into dust.

Caged, caught in the closing climax of her hour,
I still win this war of love with muscled power.
And yet as I conquer her, and conflict dies,
my slow defeat lives for a moment in her eyes.

GIVE ME TIME

The first impressions blazed harsh and clear
as the sun that sears the senses—
the stark days blistering into the brain,
the mazed recognition of you, Australia,
in your spreadeagled span of chaos.
(It takes time to learn your ways,
to breathe your air, your strange green.)
You even caught the crazed scream
from the clogged throats of the desert-lost,
the dying, in the cities who lived
between dream and death; and the cry
from the spinning limbo of lying adrift
in the sweating dark was that of terror.
(It takes time to hear your dark, the music
in the night choirs crying from the marshes.)

All I knew then, in the first hours,
was a country of shades, echoes, fadings;
a continent of empty places where man
and desert corrode the earth's green flesh;
where even the trees were tired and glum.
(It takes time to see your colours,
the brilliant shades of stone and setting sun.)
And yet there is beauty in you—
in the mirage of summer, the blowing seas,
the cicadas singing away the night hours.
So give me time to see your beauty,
breathe your strangeness, hear your melody.
Give me time to learn love.